PRAYER & STUDY GUIDE

The Power of a
PRAYING®
Wife

STORMIE
OMARTIAN

HARVEST HOUSE PUBLISHERS
EUGENE, OREGON

THE POWER OF A PRAYING® WIFE PRAYER AND STUDY GUIDE
Copyright © 2000, 2014 by Stormie Omartian
Published by Harvest House Publishers
Eugene, Oregon 97408
www.harvesthousepublishers.com

ISBN 978-0-7369-5755-7 (pbk.)
ISBN 978-0-7369-5756-4 (eBook)

Printed in the United States of America

19 20 21 22 / BP-JH / 10 9 8 7

This book belongs to

_____

Please do not read beyond this page
without permission of the person named above.

Contents

How Do I Begin?

Welcome to this great adventure of becoming a praying wife. Don't worry if you have mixed emotions during this process. We all do. It may not be easy, but it will be rewarding. That's because *prayer works*!

What You'll Need

This *Prayer and Study Guide* is divided into a 31-week plan for use in personal or group study. You will need to have the book *The Power of a Praying Wife*. You will also need a Bible. Make sure the Bible you have is one you are not hesitant to write in.

About Your Answers

The questions in this study are sometimes very personal, and your answers should be completely honest. Therefore, keep this book in a private place. If the answers you need to write down are lengthy and have the potential to be hurtful to other people, write them in a separate notebook that you can keep private or destroy later. Your answers are not for anyone else to read or for you to be tested on. They are to help you see the truth and be able to think clearly about each area of prayer focus. They will assist you in determining exactly what you and your husband's prayer needs are, and they will show you how to pray. Try to write something for each question or direction, even if it's only one sentence.

How to Proceed

In group study, it's good to follow the order in this book so the group will have the same focus when it comes together each week. In individual study, don't feel you must continue in the same order if there are pressing issues you need to pray about right away. In every instance, however, "The Power" and chapter 1: "His Wife" must be the first chapters read before proceeding.

In a Group

In group study, after you have read the appropriate chapter in *The Power of a Praying Wife* book and answered the questions in this *Prayer and Study Guide* on your own, the leader will bring the group together and go over each question to see what insights God has given you and the other women as they feel led to share them. Although you may or may not want to share personal information in the group, please share what God is showing you and speaking to your heart when you find this happening. It's good for you to say it, and it's helpful for other people to hear.

For Clarity

When referring to God, the pronouns *Him* or *He* will be capitalized. When referring to your husband, the pronouns *him* and *he* will not be capitalized.

How to Pray a Scripture

Frequently, you will be asked to write out a specific Scripture as a prayer over your husband. To help you understand how to do that, I have included an example of how I pray Ephesians 1:17-18 over my husband. Look it up in your Bible, and then see what I have done below:

> Lord, I pray that You, the God of our Lord Jesus Christ, the Father of glory, will give to *Michael* the spirit of wisdom and revelation in the knowledge of You, so that the

eyes of *Michael's* understanding will be enlightened; so that *Michael* will know what is the hope of his calling, that *Michael* will know what are the riches of the glory of Your inheritance in the saints.

What If My Husband Doesn't Know the Lord?

The Bible says a husband and wife are one, and an unbelieving husband is sanctified by the believing wife. Because of this, the wife of an unbelieving husband can pray all the same prayers and speak the same Scriptures over him as a wife could over a believing husband, and expect to see answers to prayer. The most important and ongoing prayer, of course, is that your husband's eyes be opened to the truth of God and he be led to receive Jesus as his Savior.

Your Role

Your role is to become an intercessor for your husband. *An intercessor is one who prays for someone else and makes possible the ability of that person to respond to God.* What a great privilege to be used by God in that way!

WEEK ONE

Read "The Power" and chapter 1: "His Wife"
from *The Power of a Praying Wife.*

Remember as you answer the following questions that God already knows the truth. He is not going to be shocked or disappointed in your answers, so don't you be either. Don't condemn yourself for the areas where you need improvement. We all have them. Simply take each question before the Lord and ask Him to show you the truth and help you become the woman and wife He wants you to be. Believe me, I know how hard this chapter is, but when you get through it, the rest will be easy. What happens to your heart here will pave the way for success in seeing answers to your prayers.

1. Read Matthew 19:3-6 in your Bible. Underline verses 5-6. Do you believe that you and your husband are one in the sight of God? Are there places in your marriage where you and your husband are not working together as a team? List those areas. Write out a prayer asking God to make you and your husband more unified in these specific areas. Ask Him to show you what you can do to facilitate that unity.

_____

_____

_____

_____

_____

_____

2. Read Luke 10:19 in your Bible and underline it. You don't have authority over your husband, but whom *do* you have authority over?

_____

_____

_____

_____

_____

3. God has given you the authority to take a stand against any negative influence in your marriage. Is there any area in your marriage where you see that the enemy has gained—or is trying to gain—a stronghold? Write out a prayer asking God to break down that stronghold.

_____

_____

_____

_____

_____

_____

_____

_____

_____

_____

_____

_____

4. Are there any places in your marriage where you feel hopeless? List these below. Bring them before the Lord and confess your hopelessness. Remember, confession is not to make you feel condemned; it's to help you acknowledge your error before God so He can free you from it, and so the devil can't paralyze you with it. Write out a prayer asking God to give you the faith you need to believe that He is your hope and will answer your prayers.

_____

_____

_____

_____

_____

_____

_____

_____

5. Read Joel 2:25. What things do you see depleting life out of your marriage? What does God promise He will do when things have been eaten away from our lives?

_____

_____

_____

_____

_____

_____

_____

6. Do you believe in God's ability to heal wounds? To renew love in your heart? To restore your marriage relationship to all it should be? Why or why not?

    _____

    _____

    _____

    _____

    _____

    _____

7. Read Matthew 10:39. Do you trust God enough to answer His call to lay down your life in prayer for your husband? Why or why not? If not, write a prayer asking God to help you trust Him enough to make this commitment.

    _____

    _____

    _____

    _____

    _____

    _____

8. Read Matthew 12:25. Is there any issue over which you and your husband are seriously divided? How do you feel about it?

    _____

    _____

    _____

    _____

9. Do you have any anger, unforgiveness, hurt, or disappointment toward your husband? Explain why. Even if you have good reason for feeling the way you do, write out a prayer confessing those negative thoughts as sin and ask God to set you free from them. I know this is hard if you feel justified in your feelings, but this prayer of confession and repentance must come first before you can begin praying for your husband with a right heart and see answers to your prayers.

10. Do you ever feel like you don't want to pray for your husband? Explain why. Write out a prayer asking God to help you desire to pray for God's best to be poured out on your husband. (This may be a prayer you have to pray every day for a while, so don't worry if you haven't sensed an immediate answer.)

11. Is there anything for which you need to ask your husband to forgive you? Ask God to show you if there is anything for which you need to repent (an attitude, an action, or an area of neglect). As He reveals it, write it down. Then write out a prayer asking God to give you the courage, strength, and humility you need to ask your husband for forgiveness and to communicate your love for him and a desire to change. I know this is hard, but someone has to start taking steps that lead to healing and wholeness.

_____

_____

_____

_____

_____

_____

12. Tell your husband you are going to start praying for him every day in a new and powerful way that the Lord is showing you, and ask him to share with you any prayer requests he has. Write down what his reaction was and what requests he shared.

_____

_____

_____

_____

_____

_____

13. Do you see your husband as anything less than a beloved son of God? Explain. Write out a prayer asking God to help you see your husband through His eyes.

_____

_____

_____

_____

_____

_____

_____

14. Look up Proverbs 21:19. Are there any issues in your marriage where you find yourself registering the same complaint or criticism over and over? List those. Write out a prayer asking God to show you when to speak about each matter and when to just keep silent and pray.

_____

_____

_____

_____

_____

_____

_____

_____

_____

_____

15. Is there any sensitive matter that you know you need to speak to your husband about, but you fear what his response might be? Write out your answer in a prayer asking God to show you what you should say and when to say it. Ask God to prepare your husband's heart to hear it.

_____

_____

_____

_____

_____

_____

_____

16. Read Psalm 62:5 and underline it in your Bible. Are there any expectations you have of your husband that he is not living up to? What are they? Write out a prayer asking God to show you where your expectations of your husband don't coincide with the reality of who he is. Tell God you will put your expectations on *Him* so *He* can meet your needs.

_____

_____

_____

_____

_____

_____

_____

17. Read Ephesians 5:33. Is there any area in which you have lost respect for your husband? Write out your answer as a prayer asking God to reveal ways you may have demonstrated a lack of respect for your husband. As He reveals them to you, ask God to restore that respect and help you see your husband the way *He* sees him.

_____

_____

_____

_____

_____

_____

18. Read Galatians 5:22-23 and underline these verses in your Bible. Do you have any habitually negative ways of responding to your husband that need to be changed? What are these? Write them down. Ask God to give you revelation about this. Then write down next to them which fruit of the Spirit you need in order to eliminate that negative mind-set and habit of response.

_____

_____

_____

_____

_____

_____

19. Read Proverbs 31:10-31. Ask yourself the following questions without expecting perfection:

Are you a trustworthy wife?

        Yes &rule; Need Improvement &rule;

Are you an asset to your husband?

        Yes &rule; Need Improvement &rule;

Do you work diligently to make a home in which he can be comfortable and happy?

        Yes &rule; Need Improvement &rule;

Are you careful and wise with money?

        Yes &rule; Need Improvement &rule;

Do you take care of your physical health and appearance?

        Yes &rule; Need Improvement &rule;

Are you a giving person?

        Yes &rule; Need Improvement &rule;

Are you prepared for the future?

        Yes &rule; Need Improvement &rule;

Do you make sure your family members have their needs met?

        Yes &rule; Need Improvement &rule;

Do you generally move in wisdom?

        Yes &rule; Need Improvement &rule;

Are you always loving and kind?

        Yes &rule; Need Improvement &rule;

Is your relationship with the Lord alive, intimate, growing, and strong?

        Yes &rule; Need Improvement &rule;

Without being hard on yourself, write out a prayer asking God to help you with each area in which you need to improve, and to enable you to become the wife He wants you to be.

_____

_____

_____

_____

_____

20. Pray the prayer on pages 41-43 in *The Power of a Praying Wife*. Include all the specific needs, desires, and hopes from your own heart.

_____

_____

_____

_____

_____

Whew! You got through chapter 1. If you are like me, you will probably have to keep referring back to this chapter whenever you find your attitude less than what it should be. For months I had to keep confessing my bad attitude every time I prayed for my husband, so don't feel badly if you have to do that, too. In fact, according to the mail I have received since *The Power of a Praying Wife* first came out, we are not alone in this. So don't give up, and you *will* see good results.

WEEK TWO

Read chapter 2: "His Work" from
The Power of a Praying Wife.

1. Is your husband successful in his work? Does he need to find work? Does he need to find work that is more suitable for him? Write out your answer in a prayer asking God to open up doors of opportunity for your husband to be successful in the work God created him to do.

---

2. Does your husband have a tendency toward laziness? Work-aholism? Somewhere in between? How could his work habits improve? Write out your answer in a prayer asking God to remove any obstacles from your husband's mind or emotions that cause him to be unbalanced in his work habits.

_____

_____

_____

_____

_____

_____

_____

3. Is your husband a good provider? How could you better support his efforts to provide for his family? Explain. Write out a prayer asking God to bless the work of your husband's hands so that his work will increase and he will be rewarded accordingly.

_____

_____

_____

_____

_____

_____

_____

4. Read Ecclesiastes 3:12-13. Is your husband's work fulfilling to him? Does he enjoy the good of his labor? Why or why not? Write out a prayer asking God to help your husband find fulfillment in his work, whether it means moving him into something different than what he is doing now, or giving him a new sense of purpose about the work he already has.

_____

_____

_____

_____

_____

_____

_____

5. Is your husband living up to his potential? Are there gifts and talents in him that are not being used or are not being used to the glory of God? Does he know what his gifts and talents are? Write out your answer in a prayer asking God to open up doors for your husband which utilize the gifts God has placed in him.

_____

_____

_____

_____

_____

_____

_____

6. Read Proverbs 22:29. Has your husband been unable to excel
    in his work? Has he been properly recognized and appreciated
    for his work? Write out your answer in a prayer asking God to
    enable your husband to excel in his work and be recognized for
    it.

    _____

    _____

    _____

    _____

    _____

    _____

    _____

    _____

7. Does your husband do his work with a sense of purpose and ful-
    fillment, or with feelings of frustration, aimlessness, or unful-
    fillment? Explain. How do you think you could pray about this
    for him?

    _____

    _____

    _____

    _____

    _____

    _____

    _____

    _____

8. Does your husband get along well with his coworkers? Are the people over him happy with what he does? Is he shown respect by the people he works for and with whom he has daily interaction? Describe his work relationships in general. How could you support him in prayer?

_____

_____

_____

_____

_____

_____

9. Is there a difficult person your husband has to work with, or an unpleasant work relationship that could be depleting your husband's strength and patience? Explain. Write out a prayer asking God to transform this relationship or to change your husband's perspective and enhance his patience.

_____

_____

_____

_____

_____

_____

_____

10. Pray the prayer on page 49 in *The Power of a Praying Wife*. Include specifics about your husband's work.

WEEK THREE

Read chapter 3: "His Finances" from
The Power of a Praying Wife.

1. Is your husband a financially responsible person, or is he some-
    times irresponsible with money? How do you feel about that?
    Explain.

    _____

    _____

    _____

    _____

    _____

2. Read Luke 12:29-31. Does your husband suffer from anxiety
    about finances? Explain. In light of this verse, what should he
    be doing about it? How could you pray about this?

    _____

    _____

    _____

    _____

    _____

    _____

3. Read Malachi 3:10 in your Bible and underline it. Does your
    husband have a heart to give as God directs in this Scripture, or
    does he need to move into this area of obedience to God? Write
    out your answer in a prayer asking God to speak to your hus-
    band's heart about this matter so that he always does the right
    thing.

    _____

    _____

    _____

    _____

    _____

    _____

4. Is your husband miserly, overgenerous, or somewhere in
    between? Explain. How would you like to see that changed?
    Write out a prayer asking God to give your husband a generous
    spirit controlled by the will of God.

    _____

    _____

    _____

    _____

    _____

    _____

5. Read Psalm 41:1-3. In light of these verses, the blessings that come from giving to the poor cannot be ignored. Are there any blessings you feel you are lacking because you or your husband are not giving to the poor? Explain. Remember that if your husband doesn't disapprove of *your* giving, this speaks well for *his* generosity, too.

_____

_____

_____

_____

_____

_____

_____

6. Read Matthew 6:19-21. Is your husband's focus more on his finances or more on serving the Lord? If you don't know, ask God to show you, and write down what He reveals.

_____

_____

_____

_____

_____

_____

_____

_____

7. Do you feel your husband makes financially sound decisions? Write out your answer in a prayer asking God to give you and your husband wisdom as to how to handle your finances. Pray that neither of you will spend money irresponsibly or make poor financial choices, but that you both will have God's revelation about *all* financial decisions.

_____

_____

_____

_____

_____

_____

_____

8. Have you and your husband been financially depleted for an oppressively long time? Does it seem that every time you start to get ahead, something comes along to steal finances away? Explain and be specific. Write out a prayer asking God to end financial loss, strain, poverty, or lack of blessing in your lives. Write out a proclamation that the enemy cannot steal and rob from you and your husband any longer.

_____

_____

_____

_____

_____

_____

9. Is there anything you could do to help relieve the financial burden on your husband? Ask God to show you, and write down what He reveals. If you are working to support the family also, write out a prayer asking God to bless the work of your hands and make it fruitful.

_____

_____

_____

_____

_____

_____

_____

10. Pray the prayer on page 54 in *The Power of a Praying Wife*. Include specifics about your finances.

WEEK FOUR

Read chapter 4: "His Sexuality" from
The Power of a Praying Wife.

1. Do you feel your sexual relationship with your husband is good, not good, or somewhere in between? Write out your answer in a prayer telling God how you feel and asking Him to bless that aspect of your marriage and make it all He created it to be.

_____

_____

_____

_____

_____

_____

2. How would you like to see your sexual relationship with your husband change? Write out your answer as a prayer asking God to make it all you want it to be.

_____

_____

_____

_____

_____

3. List the top ten priorities in your life. These are the things that occupy your time, attention, and energy, such as children, work, friends, church activities, and so on. In this list, where does your relationship with your husband fall? What does this list reveal to you about your priorities?

_____

_____

_____

_____

_____

_____

4. If your husband *is* at the top of your priority list under God (where he should be), is the sexual aspect of that relationship a priority? If it hasn't been, what are the reasons for that (illness, marital strife, financial worry, emotional stress, lack of interest, busy schedule, children, exhaustion)? Write out a prayer asking God to help you make any changes necessary in order to establish your sexual relationship with your husband as the priority it should be.

_____

_____

_____

_____

_____

_____

5. Do you look forward to intimate times with your husband? Has your husband done anything that has turned you off to his physical advances? Explain. What do you believe would improve your physical relationship?

_____

_____

_____

_____

_____

_____

6. Read 1 Corinthians 7:4-5. Are you sexually available for your husband? Is he available for you? Does the frequency of sex between the two of you usually depend solely upon him? Upon you? Is the frequency with which you come together mutually agreed upon? Have you ever kept yourself from being available to him when you could have done otherwise? Write out a prayer asking God to help both of you be in complete unity about this aspect of your relationship. Confess any times you kept yourself from your husband when you could have done otherwise.

_____

_____

_____

_____

_____

_____

7. Do you ever sense frustration in your husband over your sexual relationship? What do you understand his frustration to be? What could you do to help alleviate that frustration? Write out a prayer asking God to give you revelation about that and help you to do what is necessary to make your sexual relationship with your husband better.

_____

_____

_____

_____

_____

_____

_____

8. Has your husband ever been tempted toward infidelity? Have you? Has that temptation ever been acted upon? If yes, how has this affected the way you relate to each other? If no, how do you keep yourselves from temptation? Write out a prayer asking God to protect both of you from immorality.

_____

_____

_____

_____

_____

_____

9. Do you keep yourself sexually attractive to your husband? Do you try to stay healthy, fit, clean, fragrant, attractively attired, and rested? If not, what is the reason (exhaustion, hurt feelings, depression, hopelessness, sickness, emotional fatigue)? Is there anything you could do to improve yourself physically, emotionally, mentally, or spiritually? Write out your answer as a prayer, and ask God to bless you with an inner and outer attractiveness to your husband that keeps him from being attracted to anyone else.

_____

_____

_____

_____

_____

_____

_____

_____

10. Pray the prayer on page 61 in *The Power of a Praying Wife.* Include specifics related to your intimate relationship with your husband.

WEEK FIVE

Read chapter 5: "His Affection" from
The Power of a Praying Wife.

1. Read 1 Corinthians 7:3 in your Bible and underline it. Do you feel your husband is affectionate enough toward you? Explain.

_____

_____

_____

_____

_____

_____

2. Does your husband feel you are affectionate enough toward him? If you are not sure, ask him. What could you do to improve that?

_____

_____

_____

_____

_____

_____

3. What does your husband feel is the best way for you to communicate love toward him? (Ask him if you are not certain.) Are you able to do that?

_____

_____

_____

_____

_____

_____

4. If you have children, do you feel you and your husband have modeled for them a marriage that is filled with an abundance or a lack of affection? How do you think it will affect them in their own marriages? If you have modeled a lack of affection, would you both be willing to change? Even if you don't have children, answer these questions as though you did.

_____

_____

_____

_____

_____

_____

_____

5. Write out a prayer asking God to help you and your husband demonstrate healthy affection toward one another so that your children, or other children who are in your life, will want to emulate that.

_____

_____

_____

_____

_____

_____

_____

6. Have you or your husband taken one another for granted in any way that has eroded your tendency to be affectionate toward one another? Has one of you assumed incorrectly that the other one doesn't need affection? Explain.

_____

_____

_____

_____

_____

_____

_____

7. Have other distractions caused you or your husband to not take the time necessary to show affection toward one another? What could you do to change that?

_____

_____

_____

_____

_____

_____

_____

_____

8. Read 1 Corinthians 10:24 in your Bible and underline it. In what ways could you seek your husband's well-being over your own?

_____

_____

_____

_____

_____

_____

_____

_____

_____

9. Is there some act of affection you could show toward your husband today that would pleasantly surprise and bless him? What is that? (If you can't think of anything, ask God to help you.) Are you willing to do that? Write down the results after you've done it.

_____

_____

_____

_____

_____

_____

_____

_____

10. Pray the prayer on page 66 in *The Power of a Praying Wife*. Include specifics related to you and your husband's relationship.

WEEK SIX

Read chapter 6: "His Temptations"
from The Power of a Praying Wife.

1. Read Luke 22:40 in your Bible and underline it. What does Jesus specifically direct us to do in this Scripture?

    _____

    _____

    _____

    _____

    _____

2. Is there anything in your husband's life that is a temptation to him? What is that? Write out a prayer asking God to free your husband from anything that tempts him away from God's perfect will for his life, and to keep him from any temptation in the future.

    _____

    _____

    _____

    _____

    _____

    _____

3. Is there anything in *your* life that is a temptation? What is that? Write out a prayer asking God to keep you from entering into anything that tempts you away from God's perfect will for your life.

_____

_____

_____

_____

_____

_____

_____

4. Read James 1:12. If you sense that another person is becoming a temptation to your husband, pray for this individual to be taken out of your husband's life. Whether something like this has happened to him or not, write this Scripture as a prayer over your husband, substituting his name for "the man" and for all pronouns.

_____

_____

_____

_____

_____

_____

_____

_____

_____

5. Read James 1:13-15. How are we tempted? What do our own desires produce? What is the ultimate result?

_____

_____

_____

_____

_____

_____

_____

6. Read Mark 14:38. Even if your husband is not habitually tempted by anything in particular, temptation is always a possibility for anyone, especially where our flesh is weakest. Does your husband have a weakness in the flesh that you feel *could* become a snare from the enemy? If so, what is it? If you are not aware of anything, ask God to reveal it to you. Write out a prayer asking God to protect your husband in this area.

_____

_____

_____

_____

_____

_____

_____

_____

7. Does your husband have any godly men in his life to whom he can be accountable on a regular basis? List those men below and pray that they will be a great influence on your husband. If he doesn't have that kind of men in his life, write out a prayer asking God to bring godly men into his life and enable him to develop relationships of accountability with them.

_____

_____

_____

_____

_____

_____

_____

8. Read Galatians 5:16-17. What does the flesh lust against? How can you keep from fulfilling the lust of the flesh? Write out a prayer asking God to help you and your husband walk in the Spirit and not in the flesh.

_____

_____

_____

_____

_____

_____

_____

9. If your husband were to fall into some kind of temptation even after you have been praying about that, what do you think your reaction might be? What would you *want* your reaction to be? Write out your answer as a prayer asking God to keep your husband strong enough to reject all temptation, but also to give you the right reaction to any moment of weakness he succumbs to. This is a difficult prayer, but so necessary to keeping a marriage together and not allowing the enemy to steal it from you.

    _____

    _____

    _____

    _____

    _____

    _____

    _____

    _____

10. Pray the prayer on page 72 in *The Power of a Praying Wife*. Include specifics related to your husband's temptations.

WEEK SEVEN

Read chapter 7: "His Mind" from
The Power of a Praying Wife.

1. Does your husband frequently experience fear, depression, or anxiety? Explain.

_____

_____

_____

_____

_____

_____

2. Does your husband ever believe lies about himself? Explain.

_____

_____

_____

_____

_____

3. Do you believe that God has given you all authority over the
    enemy on behalf of your husband? How then would you address
    the enemy regarding the lies he speaks to your husband's mind?

    _____

    _____

    _____

    _____

    _____

4. What are the two most powerful weapons against the attack of
    lies upon your husband's mind? (See page 76, last paragraph, in
    The Power of a Praying Wife.)

    _____

    _____

    _____

    _____

    _____

5. Read Hebrews 4:12. In light of this verse, how could speaking
    the Word of God in prayer over your husband help to reveal
    wrong thinking?

    _____

    _____

    _____

    _____

    _____

6. Read 2 Timothy 1:7. Write out how you might speak this verse, inserting your husband's name and claiming it as his right.

_____

_____

_____

_____

_____

7. When we praise God for the promises He gives us in His Word, it paves the way for them to come to pass. Write out a praise to God for your husband's sound mind.

_____

_____

_____

_____

_____

_____

8. Read 1 Corinthians 2:16. Write out this verse as a prayer over your husband to help him bring every thought under God's control. Thank God for what we have in Christ.

_____

_____

_____

_____

_____

9. Read Mark 12:30. Write out this Scripture as a prayer, inserting your husband's name.

    _____

    _____

    _____

    _____

    _____

    _____

    _____

10. Pray the prayer on page 78 in *The Power of a Praying Wife*. Include specifics about your husband's struggles of the mind.

WEEK EIGHT

Read chapter 8: "His Fears" from
The Power of a Praying Wife.

1. List below any fears you know your husband has. Do you share any of the same fears? Explain why.

   _____

   _____

   _____

   _____

   _____

   _____

2. Ask your husband if there are any fears he has which he would like you to pray about for him. Are there any that he mentioned which you did not put on your list above or that you were not aware of until now?

   _____

   _____

   _____

   _____

   _____

   _____

3. How have your husband's fears affected you?

    _____

    _____

    _____

    _____

    _____

    _____

4. Read 1 John 4:18. What takes away fear?

    _____

    _____

    _____

    _____

5. Who is the only one in the universe who has perfect love? Whose love should you pray will penetrate your husband's life?

    _____

    _____

    _____

    _____

    _____

6. What is the only kind of fear we are supposed to have? (See page 82, second to last paragraph, in *The Power of a Praying Wife*.)

_____

_____

_____

_____

_____

7. When you have the fear of the Lord, what does God promise to do? (See page 82, last paragraph, in *The Power of a Praying Wife*.)

_____

_____

_____

_____

_____

8. Read Psalm 27:1. When God is your strength, of whom should you be afraid? Do you believe that with all your heart?

_____

_____

_____

_____

_____

_____

_____

9. Read Psalm 34:4. In light of this Scripture, how could you pray for your husband so that he would be set free from fear?

_____

_____

_____

_____

_____

_____

10. Pray the prayer on pages 84-85 in *The Power of a Praying Wife*. Include specifics regarding your husband's fears.

WEEK NINE

Read chapter 9: "His Purpose" from
The Power of a Praying Wife.

1. Do you have a sense of what your husband's purpose in life is, or who God created him to be? What is that? If you don't know, write out a prayer below asking God to show you.

   _____

   _____

   _____

   _____

   _____

   _____

2. Does your husband have an understanding of God's call on his life? What is his understanding of it? Explain.

   _____

   _____

   _____

   _____

   _____

   _____

3. Do you feel your husband is fulfilling the call God has on his life? Is he living in the purpose for which God created him? Explain.

_____

_____

_____

_____

_____

4. How would you like to see your husband better move into what God has called him to be?

_____

_____

_____

_____

5. Read Ephesians 1:17-19. Write out these verses as a prayer over your husband, inserting his name. ("I pray that You, the God of our Lord Jesus Christ, the Father of glory, may give to (<u>husband's name</u>)...")

_____

_____

_____

_____

_____

6. Read Psalm 20:4. Write out this Scripture as a prayer over your husband.

_____

_____

_____

_____

_____

_____

_____

_____

_____

7. Have you sought God about the call on *your* life? If so, what is it? If not, write a prayer to God asking Him to reveal it to you.

_____

_____

_____

_____

_____

_____

_____

_____

_____

_____

8. The call on your life and the call on your husband's life will never be in conflict. If they seem to be, ask God to clarify that to you. It may have to do with timing. How do you see God working out His call on both of your lives? If you don't know, write out a prayer asking Him to reveal it to you.

    _____

    _____

    _____

    _____

    _____

    _____

9. If your husband is already moving in the call God has on his life, the enemy will try to cast doubt and discouragement into his soul. Do you ever see that happening? Write out a prayer asking God to silence the enemy's lies to your husband so that God's voice to his heart can be clearly heard.

    _____

    _____

    _____

    _____

    _____

    _____

10. Pray the prayer on page 90 in *The Power of a Praying Wife*. Include specifics about your husband's purpose and call.

WEEK TEN

Read chapter 10: "His Choices" from
The Power of a Praying Wife.

1. Do you feel your husband generally makes good decisions? Why or why not?

   _____

   _____

   _____

   _____

   _____

   _____

2. Do you often see or sense things instinctively that your husband doesn't? How does he react to this? Does he see or sense things that you don't? How do you react to this?

   _____

   _____

   _____

   _____

   _____

3. Does your husband ask your advice before making major deci-
    sions or choices with significant ramifications? Why or why not?
    How do you feel about that?

    _____

    _____

    _____

    _____

    _____

    _____

    _____

    _____

4. When you give your husband advice, does he weigh it carefully
    before making any major decision or choice? How does that
    make you feel? How can your prayers help him to make wise
    choices?

    _____

    _____

    _____

    _____

    _____

    _____

    _____

    _____

5. Read Proverbs 1:7. Does your husband seek God before making decisions? Does he wait for God's leading before acting? Explain. What does this Scripture say he should do and why?

_____

_____

_____

_____

_____

6. Read Proverbs 1:5. Write out this Scripture as a prayer over your husband, inserting his name.

_____

_____

_____

_____

_____

7. Is there any area in which you feel your husband consistently makes poor choices? Explain. Write out a prayer asking God to help him learn to seek the leading of the Lord first and make better choices in that area.

_____

_____

_____

_____

_____

8. Read Proverbs 11:14. Are there godly people with whom your husband could seek counsel regarding certain decisions he has to make? Who are they? If you cannot think of anyone, write out a prayer asking God to send godly counselors into your husband's life.

    _____

    _____

    _____

    _____

    _____

    _____

9. Write out a prayer asking God to help the godly counselors in your husband's life to always impart understanding and direction to him. Pray also that he will receive it.

    _____

    _____

    _____

    _____

    _____

    _____

10. Pray the prayer on page 95 in *The Power of a Praying Wife*. Add specifics related to your husband's choices.

WEEK ELEVEN

Read chapter 11: "His Health" from
The Power of a Praying Wife.

1. How would you describe your husband's general health?

   _____

   _____

   _____

2. Are there specific areas of your husband's health that concern you?

   _____

   _____

   _____

3. Are there any specific areas of your husband's physical health that you are concerned about possibly being a problem in the future? Explain.

   _____

   _____

   _____

   _____

   _____

4. Does your husband have good or bad habits when it comes to taking care of his health? Describe and be specific.

_____

_____

_____

_____

5. Does your husband have good intentions but poor follow-through, good intentions and good follow-through, or does he have no intentions at all when it comes to taking care of his health? Describe.

_____

_____

_____

_____

6. Does your husband have particular habits that bother you because they undermine his health? Explain what they are. Would you describe your attitude about his health habits as being pleasantly patient, cheerfully convicting, or notoriously nagging? Explain.

_____

_____

_____

_____

_____

7. Are there things you have tried to get your husband to do for his health, but he just won't do them? What are they? How does that make you feel when he won't take your suggestions to heart? What do you think he should be doing for his health?

_____

_____

_____

_____

_____

_____

_____

_____

8. Read Proverbs 16:24. In light of this Scripture, how can you contribute to your husband's health?

_____

_____

_____

_____

_____

_____

_____

9. Read 2 Kings 20:5. What does this Scripture promise to those who pray fervently?

    _____

    _____

    _____

    _____

    _____

10. Pray the prayer on page 99 in *The Power of a Praying Wife*. Include specifics about your husband's health habits.

WEEK TWELVE

Read chapter 12: "His Protection" from
The Power of a Praying Wife.

1. Have you heard of or experienced incidents where you or a person you know was saved from disaster because someone had prayed? Give an example.

   _____

   _____

   _____

   _____

   _____

2. Do you believe God will answer your prayers for protection on your husband? Why do you believe that?

   _____

   _____

   _____

   _____

   _____

3. Read Psalm 61:3. Write out this Scripture as a prayer for your husband, inserting his name. (For example, "Lord, I pray You will be a shelter for (<u>husband's name</u>)...")

_____

_____

_____

_____

_____

_____

_____

_____

_____

4. Read Psalm 91:11-12. Write out these verses as a prayer for your husband, inserting his name.

_____

_____

_____

_____

_____

_____

5. Do you see any possible dangers in your husband's life that need to be covered in prayer (travel in cars or airplanes, or dangers at work)? List them below. Be specific.

_____

_____

_____

_____

_____

_____

6. Does your husband ever do anything that you consider unnecessarily dangerous? Do you feel he needs to be more careful or stop taking risks? Do you sense dangers that he is not concerned about? How do you feel God is leading you to pray about the situation?

_____

_____

_____

_____

_____

7. Read Psalm 91:1-2. Write out these verses as a prayer over your husband, inserting his name.

_____

_____

_____

_____

8. Read Psalm 18:3. In light of this Scripture, how are you and your husband protected from the enemy?

_____

_____

_____

_____

_____

_____

9. Do you believe that when you call upon the Lord He will hear your prayers and save you and your husband from your enemies? Why or why not?

_____

_____

_____

_____

_____

_____

10. Read the prayer on page 103 in *The Power of a Praying Wife*. Include specifics about the protection of your husband.

WEEK THIRTEEN

Read chapter 13: "His Trials" from
The Power of a Praying Wife.

1. Read James 1:2-3. Does your husband find joy in the midst of trials? How does he react to tough times?

_____

_____

_____

_____

_____

_____

2. Do you believe your prayers can make a difference in how your husband responds to trials? How so?

_____

_____

_____

_____

_____

_____

_____

3. Read Romans 8:28. Do you really believe that? Why or why not? Is your faith strong enough to help your husband find the good in tough times? Are you willing to pray him through any trial? Why or why not?

_____

_____

_____

_____

_____

_____

_____

4. God uses trials to work His purposes in our lives. How can you pray for your husband to not be destroyed in the trials he faces without minimizing what God desires to accomplish in him through them? (See page 107 in *The Power of a Praying Wife.*)

_____

_____

_____

_____

_____

_____

_____

_____

5. Is there a certain kind of trial that keeps reoccurring in your husband's life? What is that (problem with work, finances, relationships)?

_____

_____

_____

_____

_____

_____

6. Read Psalm 55:16-17. How often do you need to pray when you are in the heat of a battle or trial?

_____

_____

_____

_____

7. Read Matthew 24:13. Write out a prayer for your husband based on that Scripture.

_____

_____

_____

_____

_____

8. Is your husband in the midst of a trial right now? What is it? How can you support him in prayer?

_____

_____

_____

_____

_____

_____

9. Read 1 Peter 1:6-7. Write out this Scripture as a prayer, inserting your husband's name.

_____

_____

_____

_____

_____

_____

10. Pray the prayer on pages 108-109 in *The Power of a Praying Wife*. Include specifics about any trial your husband is facing.

WEEK FOURTEEN

Read chapter 14: "His Integrity" from
The Power of a Praying Wife.

1. Integrity means to adhere to moral and ethical principles. Do you feel your husband is a man of integrity? Why or why not?

    _____

    _____

    _____

    _____

    _____

    _____

2. Is the man your husband appears to be to other people the same or different than the man you know him to be in private? How so?

    _____

    _____

    _____

    _____

    _____

    _____

3. Is your husband, for the most part, a man of his word? Could he improve in that area? If so, in what way?

_____

_____

_____

_____

_____

_____

4. Read John 16:13. In light of this Scripture, how can you pray for moral and ethical guidance for your husband?

_____

_____

_____

_____

_____

5. Read Proverbs 20:7. In light of this Scripture, what is another important reason to pray for your husband's integrity?

_____

_____

_____

_____

_____

6. Is your husband easily deceived? Have you ever seen him being deceived in any way? Are you concerned that he might be deceived sometime in the future? Explain. Write out a prayer below, asking God to open your husband's eyes to the truth so that the enemy will not be able to blind him.

_____

_____

_____

_____

_____

_____

_____

7. Do you believe your husband would ever compromise what he knows to be the right thing to do? Write out your answer in a prayer about that.

_____

_____

_____

_____

_____

_____

_____

8. Do you sense there are influences around your husband try-
    ing to sway him away from the paths of righteousness? Identify
    those influences and write out a prayer for the removal of them
    from his life.

    _____

    _____

    _____

    _____

    _____

    _____

9. Any man can be bombarded by the enemy seeking to destroy
    him. Write a proclamation in Jesus' name that the enemy of
    your husband's soul will have no power to sway him from moral
    principles he knows are right.

    _____

    _____

    _____

    _____

    _____

    _____

10. Pray the prayer on page 113 in *The Power of a Praying Wife*.
    Include specifics about your husband's integrity.

WEEK FIFTEEN

Read chapter 15: "His Reputation"
from *The Power of a Praying Wife.*

1. Read Proverbs 22:1. Why do you think God puts such a high value on having a good reputation?

_____

_____

_____

_____

_____

_____

_____

2. What are three ways our reputations can be ruined? (See page 115, second paragraph, in *The Power of a Praying Wife*.)

_____

_____

_____

_____

_____

_____

_____

3. Have any of the three ways mentioned previously happened to you and/or your husband? Explain.

    _____

    _____

    _____

    _____

    _____

4. Do you feel your and/or your husband's reputations have been damaged? How so? How do you feel about that? Do you believe God can restore your good name?

    _____

    _____

    _____

    _____

    _____

5. If you feel that your or your husband's reputations have been damaged in any way, write a prayer asking God to redeem and restore your good names. Whether anything like that has happened to you or not, write out a prayer asking God to keep this kind of situation from happening to you in the future.

    _____

    _____

    _____

    _____

    _____

6. Read Proverbs 31:23. Do you think a virtuous wife automatically deserves a husband who is respected, or does she have an important part to play in that happening? What part could she play?

_____

_____

_____

_____

_____

_____

_____

7. Read Psalm 17:8-9. In these days of lawsuits, it is worth your time and effort to pray that such things never bring destruction upon you or your husband. How could you pray the above verses over you and your husband?

_____

_____

_____

_____

_____

_____

_____

_____

8. Gossip can destroy reputations quickly. Write out a prayer asking God to protect you and your husband from it.

_____

_____

_____

_____

_____

_____

9. If damaging gossip has already been spread about you or your husband, write out a prayer asking God to silence those voices and be your Defender. Ask Him to bring restoration and help you and your husband to forgive the people who gossiped.

_____

_____

_____

_____

_____

_____

10. Pray the prayer on pages 117-118 in *The Power of a Praying Wife*. Include specifics about your husband's reputation.

WEEK SIXTEEN

Read chapter 16: "His Priorities" from
The Power of a Praying Wife.

1. Read Matthew 4:10. What should be the top priority in your husband's life? In your life?

    _____

    _____

    _____

2. Do you feel your husband's priorities are in the right order? Explain.

    _____

    _____

    _____

    _____

3. Do you believe that you are first, after God, on your husband's priority list? Explain.

    _____

    _____

    _____

    _____

4. Do you ever feel that you are unprotected, unloved, or uncovered because you are not a priority with your husband? Why or why not? Write out a prayer asking God to heal any hurts in this area.

_____

_____

_____

_____

_____

5. Can you think of ways you could set aside time for you and your husband to be alone, doing something he would enjoy? Write down those ideas.

_____

_____

_____

_____

_____

6. Do you ever wish your husband would take time for you alone more than he does? Explain.

_____

_____

_____

_____

_____

7. Do you ever feel your husband puts his children before you? In what way?

_____

_____

_____

_____

8. Does your husband ever feel you put your children before him? (Ask him if you are not sure.) If so, what could you do about this? Ask God to help you make your husband feel that he is very important to you.

_____

_____

_____

_____

9. Read Philippians 2:4. Does your husband look out for the interests of his family before himself? Do you feel he puts the interests of other people before those of his own family? Explain. How does that affect your family? Write out a prayer about it.

_____

_____

_____

_____

10. Pray the prayer on page 123 in *The Power of a Praying Wife*. Include specifics about your husband's priorities.

WEEK SEVENTEEN

Read chapter 17: "His Relationships"
from *The Power of a Praying Wife*.

1. What are your husband's friends like? Are they godly? Do you feel they are an asset to him or a detriment? Explain.

   _____

   _____

   _____

   _____

   _____

   _____

2. Read Proverbs 12:26. Are there any people you would consider to be especially bad influences in your husband's life? Does he have any relationships that continually trouble him? Explain.

   _____

   _____

   _____

   _____

   _____

   _____

3. Read 2 Corinthians 6:14. Does your husband have any close friends or close business relationships with people who are not believers? List their names below and pray for their salvation.

_____

_____

_____

_____

_____

4. Where does your husband find most of his friends (church, work, athletic clubs)? Do you think it is a good place to meet the kinds of friends he needs?

_____

_____

_____

_____

_____

5. Does your husband have close, mature, believing male friends or mentors who counsel him and encourage his spiritual growth? Does he want men like that in his life?

_____

_____

_____

_____

_____

6. Does your husband have a good relationship with each of his family members? Is there anyone in particular who is especially troubling for him? Are some family relationships weak or strained? Write out a prayer about those relationships.

———————————————————————————————

———————————————————————————————

———————————————————————————————

———————————————————————————————

———————————————————————————————

———————————————————————————————

———————————————————————————————

7. Is your husband part of a men's prayer group or Bible study? If yes, write out a prayer concerning his involvement in that group. If no, write out a prayer for that to become a reality in his life, no matter how remote that possibility may seem now.

———————————————————————————————

———————————————————————————————

———————————————————————————————

———————————————————————————————

———————————————————————————————

———————————————————————————————

———————————————————————————————

8. Is there any relationship your husband has that is strained or broken because of his unforgiveness? Explain. Write out a prayer asking God to convict your husband's heart about his need to forgive.

    _____

    _____

    _____

    _____

    _____

    _____

9. How is your friendship with your husband? Do you think it could be improved upon or deepened? How could you pray to that end?

    _____

    _____

    _____

    _____

    _____

    _____

10. Pray the prayer on pages 128-129 in *The Power of a Praying Wife.* Include specifics about your husband's relationships.

WEEK EIGHTEEN

Read chapter 18: "His Fatherhood"
from *The Power of a Praying Wife.*

1. Does your husband ever worry about being a good father? Have you asked him if he does? If he has never been a father, does he want to be? Explain.

_____

_____

_____

_____

_____

2. Did your husband have a good father? What does he say his relationship with his father was like? What is it like today? If his father is not around, for whatever reason, what is your husband's attitude toward the father he had?

_____

_____

_____

_____

_____

_____

3. Does your husband desire to emulate his father as a dad, or does he want to do a better job with his children than his father did with him? Explain.

_____

_____

_____

_____

_____

_____

_____

4. Does your husband have a good relationship with each of his children? Why or why not? If he does not have children of his own, does he get along well with other people's children? Does he need prayer about that?

_____

_____

_____

_____

_____

_____

_____

_____

5. Do you feel your husband has bonded with each child? Do you feel you have bonded with each of your children? If you do not have children, explain how you feel about this situation and how you would like to see your prayers answered regarding it.

_____

_____

_____

_____

_____

_____

_____

6. Does your husband ever feel guilty or like he has failed as a parent when he sees something wrong with his children? Explain. If he does not have children, does he feel a lack because of it? How could you pray about that?

_____

_____

_____

_____

_____

_____

_____

_____

7. What is the best way for a man to become a good father? What is the best way to have a father's heart? (See page 133, first paragraph, in *The Power of a Praying Wife*.)

_____

_____

_____

_____

_____

_____

_____

_____

8. Read 2 Corinthians 6:18. Does your husband really know God as his heavenly Father? Do you? Explain. Write out a prayer asking God to reveal Himself to you both as your heavenly Father.

_____

_____

_____

_____

_____

_____

_____

_____

_____

9. Do you ever feel your husband is more concerned with being a good father than he is with being a good husband? Explain. How does that make you feel?

_____

_____

_____

_____

_____

_____

_____

10. Pray the prayer on pages 135-136 in *The Power of a Praying Wife*. Include specifics about your husband's ability to be a good father.

WEEK NINETEEN

Read chapter 19: "His Past" from
The Power of a Praying Wife.

1. Is there anything from your husband's past that repeatedly torments him? Describe.

    _____

    _____

    _____

    _____

    _____

    _____

2. Is your husband's past a part of his life he tries to ignore, something from which he learns, or a place where he lives? Explain.

    _____

    _____

    _____

    _____

    _____

    _____

    _____

3. Read Philippians 3:13-14. Do you feel your husband is able to reach forward to all God has for him? How do you think your prayers might help him to do that? Write out these verses as a prayer for your husband.

_____

_____

_____

_____

_____

_____

_____

_____

4. Are you concerned that there is anything from your husband's past that could be passed down to your children (alcoholism, divorce, anger, fear, lust)? Explain.

_____

_____

_____

_____

_____

_____

_____

_____

5. Was there anything that happened in your husband's childhood that is affecting his life today? Was his childhood happy, sad, troubled, carefree, normal, uneventful, full of turmoil, or unstable? Explain.

_____

_____

_____

_____

_____

_____

_____

6. Was your husband ever labeled with unflattering names that have imprinted themselves on his memory and emotions and perhaps colored his image of himself? Explain. Write out a prayer breaking the power of those hurtful memories and asking God to heal the wounds.

_____

_____

_____

_____

_____

_____

_____

7. Read 2 Corinthians 5:17. Does your husband truly understand that he is a new creature in the Lord? Do you? Explain why you do or do not believe this truth. Write out a prayer asking God to help both you and your husband fully understand and believe this promise of Scripture.

_____

_____

_____

_____

_____

_____

_____

_____

8. Read Isaiah 43:18-19. Write out below what you are to do about the past. What does God promise if you do that? Do you believe this for your husband? For yourself?

_____

_____

_____

_____

_____

_____

_____

_____

9. Read Ephesians 4:22-24. Write out these verses as a prayer, inserting your husband's name. Then do the same thing putting in your name.

_____

_____

_____

_____

_____

_____

_____

_____

10. Pray the prayer on page 142 in *The Power of a Praying Wife*. Include specifics about your husband's past (and your past, too).

WEEK TWENTY

Read chapter 20: "His Attitude" from
The Power of a Praying Wife.

1. Does your husband frequently have a bad attitude, or is he usually even-tempered and cheerful? Explain.

    _____

    _____

    _____

    _____

    _____

2. Do events of the day affect your husband's attitude, or is he able to rise above them and cast his cares on the Lord with ease? Explain.

    _____

    _____

    _____

    _____

    _____

3. Do you react to negativity in your husband? How so? Do you
    immediately go to the Lord in prayer about it? How could you
    respond more positively?

    _____

    _____

    _____

    _____

    _____

    _____

    _____

4. Has your husband's attitude affected you as a person? How so?
    Have negative attitudes been brought out in you as a result of
    his reactions? Explain.

    _____

    _____

    _____

    _____

    _____

    _____

    _____

5. Has your husband's attitude affected your marriage in a negative way or a positive way? Explain. How could you pray about that?

_____

_____

_____

_____

_____

_____

_____

_____

6. Read 1 Corinthians 13:2-3. Do you believe your husband has truly experienced God's love in his life? Do you feel he has the love of God in his heart? What can we accomplish without the love of God in our heart?

_____

_____

_____

_____

_____

_____

_____

7. Read Psalm 100:4-5. Does your husband know how to do what is described here? Write out these verses as a prayer, inserting your husband's name. Then write it again, inserting your name.

_____

_____

_____

_____

_____

_____

_____

_____

_____

8. Read Proverbs 15:13. In light of this Scripture, how could you pray for your husband's attitude?

_____

_____

_____

_____

_____

_____

9. Read Matthew 12:35. Do you see good things or bad things coming from your husband's heart? How can this Scripture inspire you to pray over your husband?

_____

_____

_____

_____

_____

_____

_____

_____

10. Pray the prayer on page 147 in *The Power of a Praying Wife*. Include specifics about your husband's attitude.

WEEK TWENTY-ONE

Read chapter 21: "His Marriage" from
The Power of a Praying Wife.

1. Have you or your husband ever been divorced? If so, write a prayer breaking the spirit of divorce over your lives. If not, write out a prayer that a spirit of divorce will never enter into your marriage.

   _____

   _____

   _____

   _____

2. Is there divorce in your husband's family, especially with his parents or grandparents? Explain. Write out a prayer breaking any generational tie that would cause a spirit of divorce to become part of his life.

   _____

   _____

   _____

   _____

   _____

   _____

3. Is there divorce in *your* family, especially with your parents or grandparents? Explain. Write out a prayer breaking any generational tie that would cause a spirit of divorce to become part of your life.

    _____

    _____

    _____

    _____

    _____

    _____

4. Read 1 Corinthians 7:10-11. Have you or your husband ever viewed divorce as an option which you would consider? Explain. Write out a prayer breaking the power of those thoughts of divorce.

    _____

    _____

    _____

    _____

    _____

    _____

    _____

    _____

5. Has your husband ever committed adultery during your marriage or any previous marriage? If so, write out a prayer asking God to deliver him from all the bondage of that sin. If not, pray for the protection, strength, and grace to keep him from ever falling into anything like that—even in thought.

_____

_____

_____

_____

_____

6. Have you committed adultery, even in thought, during your marriage or any previous marriage? If yes, write out a prayer of repentance before the Lord and ask for His forgiveness and deliverance from the bondage of that sin. If no, write out a prayer asking for the strength, grace, and protection to keep you from ever falling into anything like that—even in thought.

_____

_____

_____

_____

_____

_____

_____

7. Read 1 Corinthians 10:12. In light of this Scripture, what should you never assume? How does this Scripture inspire you to keep praying for the strength of your marriage?

_____

_____

_____

_____

_____

_____

_____

8. Is there any person or thing that threatens the stability of your marriage? Write out a sentence below, taking authority over that threat in Jesus' name and commanding it to be removed from your life. If there is nothing threatening your marriage, write out a prayer asking God for protection over your marriage so no person or situation will ever be allowed to threaten or harm it.

_____

_____

_____

_____

_____

_____

_____

9. Make a statement below, declaring to the enemy that you refuse to allow anything to come in and destroy your marriage. Declare to God that you will partner with Him and do whatever it takes as far as you are concerned to see that your marriage becomes all it is supposed to be.

    _____

    _____

    _____

    _____

    _____

    _____

10. Pray the prayer on page 152 in *The Power of a Praying Wife*. Include the specifics of your marriage.

WEEK TWENTY-TWO

Read chapter 22: "His Emotions" from
The Power of a Praying Wife.

1. Is there a negative emotion that you commonly observe in your husband? If so, what is it (anger, depression, fear, and so on)? How does it manifest itself?

_____

_____

_____

_____

_____

2. Read Proverbs 22:24-25. What can happen when we are frequently around someone with a constant negative emotion? (In this example, it's anger.)

_____

_____

_____

_____

_____

3. Do you see from the previous Scripture how important it is for your own well-being, as well as your husband's, to pray for his emotions? Describe how his emotions affect yours.

_____

_____

_____

_____

_____

_____

4. It's good to pray that your husband will stop being controlled by his emotions and instead be controlled by what? (See page 155, second paragraph, in *The Power of a Praying Wife*.)

_____

_____

_____

_____

5. Read Proverbs 21:14. What is the best gift a wife can secretly give her husband? (See page 155, second paragraph, in *The Power of a Praying Wife*.)

_____

_____

_____

_____

_____

6. Do you have any negative emotions that are frequently reoccurring? If so, what are they? Why do you think you have them? How could you pray about them?

_____

_____

_____

_____

_____

_____

_____

_____

_____

7. How do your negative emotions affect your husband? What could you do to not be controlled by your emotions?

_____

_____

_____

_____

_____

_____

_____

_____

_____

8. Read Psalm 34:1-4. From these verses, what is it we should be doing to combat anger, depression, and fear? How often are we to praise Him?

    _____

    _____

    _____

    _____

    _____

    _____

9. Read Psalm 23:3. In light of this Scripture, are negative emotions part of a person's character that cannot be changed? Explain.

    _____

    _____

    _____

    _____

    _____

10. Pray the prayer on page 157 in *The Power of a Praying Wife*. Include specifics about your husband's emotions (yours, too).

WEEK TWENTY-THREE

Read chapter 23: "His Walk" from
The Power of a Praying Wife.

1. How would you describe the kind of walk your husband has
   through life? Does he walk close with God or independently
   from God?

   _____

   _____

   _____

   _____

   _____

   _____

2. Does your husband have a sense of direction and purpose, or
   does he wander aimlessly, or somewhere in between? Explain.

   _____

   _____

   _____

   _____

   _____

   _____

3. Read Psalm 84:11. What are the rewards for those who walk in righteousness before God?

_____

_____

_____

_____

4. Read Psalm 1:1-2; 128:1; Proverbs 10:9; 13:20. According to these Scriptures, how are we supposed to walk?

_____

_____

_____

_____

5. Faith and obedience get us on the Highway of Holiness, but in order to stay on that path we are supposed to walk in the_____ and not in the_____? (See page 160, second paragraph, in *The Power of a Praying Wife*.) Which do you believe your husband walks in most of the time? Why?

_____

_____

_____

_____

_____

_____

6. Do you trust your husband to walk righteously, or do you fear he can easily be led off the right path? Explain why you feel the way you do.

_____

_____

_____

_____

_____

_____

_____

_____

7. Read Romans 8:5-9. How can we live according to the Spirit? What happens when we live in the flesh? How can you be sure that you are not walking in the flesh?

_____

_____

_____

_____

_____

_____

_____

_____

_____

8. Read Romans 8:13-14. What is the ultimate end of living in the flesh? Of living in the Spirit?

    _____

    _____

    _____

    _____

    _____

    _____

9. Read Jeremiah 10:23. From this Scripture, describe how we are to walk through our lives. How then should you pray for your husband's walk?

    _____

    _____

    _____

    _____

    _____

    _____

10. Pray the prayer on page 161 in *The Power of a Praying Wife*. Include specifics as related to your husband's walk with God.

WEEK TWENTY-FOUR

Read chapter 24: "His Talk" from
The Power of a Praying Wife.

1. Read Ecclesiastes 10:12. Do you feel the words that come from your husband's mouth are generally good or sometimes foolish? Have his words ever hurt you? Have you had to forgive him for his words? Explain.

_____

_____

_____

_____

_____

_____

2. Read Ephesians 4:29. Write this Scripture as a prayer over your husband.

_____

_____

_____

_____

_____

_____

3. Do you feel your husband is a man of truth? To what degree is he or isn't he? Explain.

    _____

    _____

    _____

    _____

    _____

    _____

    _____

    _____

4. Read Psalm 34:12-13. In light of these verses, what is a good reason to pray for your husband to be a man who speaks truth?

    _____

    _____

    _____

    _____

    _____

    _____

    _____

    _____

    _____

    _____

5. Is your husband a complainer? Does he always see the glass half empty or half full? Explain. Write out a prayer asking God to give him a sense of hope, peace, and joy.

    _____

    _____

    _____

    _____

    _____

    _____

    _____

6. Does your husband speak too quickly before he thinks or weighs the consequences of his words? How do his words reveal what's in his heart? Explain. How could you pray about that?

    _____

    _____

    _____

    _____

    _____

    _____

    _____

    _____

    _____

    _____

7. Read Matthew 12:37 and 15:11. Have you ever seen your husband's words bring negative results into his own life? Explain.

_____

_____

_____

_____

_____

_____

_____

_____

_____

8. Read Proverbs 15:23. What can we derive from the words we speak? Does your husband need more of that in his life? Do you?

_____

_____

_____

_____

_____

_____

9. Read Proverbs 13:3. What is the ultimate consequence of not watching what you say? How could you pray this Scripture over your husband? How could you pray it over yourself?

_____

_____

_____

_____

_____

_____

_____

_____

_____

10. Pray the prayer on page 165 in *The Power of a Praying Wife*. Include specifics about your husband's talk.

WEEK TWENTY-FIVE

Read chapter 25: "His Repentance"
from *The Power of a Praying Wife*.

1. Read Proverbs 28:13. Does your husband have difficulty confessing his faults? What will happen if he doesn't confess his sins? What will happen when he does confess his sins?

    _____

    _____

    _____

    _____

    _____

    _____

2. When your husband confesses his faults, do you feel he is truly repentant and intent on changing his behavior? Explain why or why not.

    _____

    _____

    _____

    _____

    _____

    _____

3. What are the three steps to changing our behavior? (See page 167, third paragraph, in *The Power of a Praying Wife*.)

First there is _____ , which is _____

_____ .

Second there is _____ , which is _____

_____ .

Third there is _____ , which is _____

_____ .

4. What does true repentance mean? (See page 168, first paragraph.)

_____

_____

_____

_____

5. Do you feel your husband moves fully in those steps of confession, repentance, and asking forgiveness? With which step does he have the most difficulty? The least difficulty? How could you pray about that? Answer these same questions about yourself.

_____

_____

_____

_____

_____

_____

6. Read Romans 2:4. What leads us to repentance? What will lead your husband to repentance? What will lead *you* to repentance? How could you pray about that?

    _____

    _____

    _____

    _____

    _____

    _____

    _____

7. Does pride ever keep your husband from admitting he is wrong? Do you feel this may have kept him from some of the blessings God has for him? Explain. Write out a prayer breaking any stronghold of pride in your husband. Then do the same for yourself.

    _____

    _____

    _____

    _____

    _____

    _____

    _____

    _____

    _____

8. Are there instances where you believe your husband's true repentance would bring needed healing to your relationship? How could you pray about that?

    _____

    _____

    _____

    _____

    _____

    _____

9. Read 1 John 3:21-22. How will admitting your sins ultimately affect you or your husband?

    _____

    _____

    _____

    _____

    _____

10. Pray the prayer on page 169 in *The Power of a Praying Wife*. Include specifics as related to your husband's repentance.

WEEK TWENTY-SIX

Read chapter 26: "His Deliverance"
from *The Power of a Praying Wife*.

1. Is there anything in your husband's life from which you know
   he needs to be set free (alcohol, drugs, pornography, lust, eating
   disorder)? Explain.

   _____

   _____

   _____

   _____

   _____

   _____

2. Read Psalm 50:15. What do you have to do to see God's deliverance happen in your life? Does your husband believe that Jesus
   is his Deliverer? Do you?

   _____

   _____

   _____

   _____

   _____

   _____

3. Read Proverbs 24:11. Does your husband ever do things that seem self-destructive, careless, or dangerous? Explain.

_____

_____

_____

_____

_____

_____

_____

_____

4. Does your husband ever feel hopeless, as if there is no way out of a situation? In what kinds of situations does he feel that? Explain.

_____

_____

_____

_____

_____

_____

_____

_____

5. The ultimate result of feeling that there is no way out is suicide. Has your husband ever had suicidal thoughts? If so, how often and how serious were they? Whether he has had those thoughts or not, write out a prayer asking God to keep him free from any suicidal thoughts in the future.

    _____

    _____

    _____

    _____

    _____

    _____

    _____

6. Read Psalm 91:14. Often simply by setting our sights on the Lord, having a heart for Him, and living His way, deliverance will happen. How could you pray this Scripture over your husband, trusting that deliverance will happen for him?

    _____

    _____

    _____

    _____

    _____

    _____

    _____

7. Everything from which we need deliverance comes from the enemy. State here again what you have been given over the power of the enemy (Luke 10:19). How do you intend to use that knowledge to see your husband set free from things that control him? How do you intend to use it for your own deliverance?

_____

_____

_____

_____

_____

_____

8. Don't hesitate to take dominion over the enemy and proclaim that you will not allow his plans to succeed in your husband's life, because you are praying that only the Lord's plans will succeed. Write that below and be sure to state in whose name you have been given authority to make that statement. Do the same for yourself as well.

_____

_____

_____

_____

_____

_____

9. Read Galatians 5:1. Because you are one with your husband, you can stand strong with him to resist the power of the enemy whenever the enemy seeks to put him into bondage. How can you pray for your husband regarding this Scripture?

_____

_____

_____

_____

_____

_____

_____

10. Pray the prayer on page 173 in *The Power of a Praying Wife*. Name the specific things from which your husband needs deliverance.

WEEK TWENTY-SEVEN

Read chapter 27: "His Obedience"
from *The Power of a Praying Wife*.

1. Do you feel your husband has as deep and committed a relationship with God as you do? Or is it deeper and more committed than yours? Of the two of you, who do you feel needs the most spiritual growth in order to catch up with the other? Write out a prayer asking God to help you grow together in the Lord.

_____

_____

_____

_____

_____

2. Do you consider your husband a man of prayer? How much does he pray? Would you like to see him pray more? Write out a prayer about that.

_____

_____

_____

_____

_____

3. Do you feel that your husband has a heart to obey God and live His way? Explain.

_____

_____

_____

_____

_____

_____

_____

4. Do you ever see your husband doing things that are opposed to the way God has asked us to live? Do you speak to him about those things? If so, how does he respond? How can you pray for him about this?

_____

_____

_____

_____

_____

_____

_____

_____

5. Do you believe that praying for your husband first before saying anything, or just praying and not saying anything at all, could have a positive effect on his ability to change? How so? Explain.

---

6. One of the best ways to learn how God wants us to live is to read His Word. Does your husband read the Bible regularly? Does he get good Bible teaching? Write out a prayer below asking God to open your husband's heart to an ever-increasing knowledge of the truth of His Word.

---

7.   Read Matthew 7:24-27. In light of these verses, how important
is it to you and your family that your husband obeys God?

_____

_____

_____

_____

_____

_____

_____

8.   Read Proverbs 28:9. What happens when we don't walk in obedience? Does your husband experience frustration over unan-
swered prayer? In light of this Scripture, what could be a possible
reason?

_____

_____

_____

_____

_____

_____

_____

_____

9. Read Proverbs 29:18. When we don't have revelation, we get careless. Bad things happen to people because they have no revelation and as a result throw caution to the wind. When we have revelation, we see the wisdom of walking in a manner totally dependent upon God and of living God's way every moment. Write out a prayer below asking God to give your husband that kind of revelation and a desire to obey Him.

_____

_____

_____

_____

_____

_____

_____

_____

10. Pray the prayer on page 178 in *The Power of a Praying Wife*. Include specifics as related to your husband's obedience.

WEEK TWENTY-EIGHT

Read chapter 28: "His Self-Image"
from *The Power of a Praying Wife*.

1. Do you feel that your husband is living up to his potential? Why or why not?

_____

_____

_____

_____

_____

_____

2. Is your husband's perception of himself that of a successful man, or does he have doubts about himself that creep into his job performance? Explain.

_____

_____

_____

_____

_____

_____

3. Does your husband have feelings of rejection? Did he feel rejected in his past? Does he feel rejected by you? His children? His family members? Does he commonly anticipate being rejected by people? Explain.

    _____

    _____

    _____

    _____

    _____

    _____

    _____

4. Does rejection run in your husband's family? Are his family members easily made to feel rejected? Have there been misunderstandings because he or a family member feels rejected? Explain.

    _____

    _____

    _____

    _____

    _____

    _____

5. Do *you* ever have feelings of rejection? Do you ever feel rejected by your husband? Is rejection a part of your past? Explain.

_____

_____

_____

_____

_____

_____

_____

_____

_____

_____

6. Read Ephesians 1:3-6. Write out these verses as a prayer for you and your husband. (For example, "Thank You, Lord, that You have blessed us with…")

_____

_____

_____

_____

_____

_____

_____

_____

_____

7. Part of being accepted by other people has to do with accepting who we are in the Lord first. Do you feel your husband accepts himself, or is he hard on himself? Explain. Do you accept yourself or are you hard on yourself?

_____

_____

_____

_____

_____

_____

_____

8. Write out a prayer below asking God to help your husband fully receive love and acceptance from the Lord and be able to find his identity in Him as well.

_____

_____

_____

_____

_____

_____

9. Read Colossians 3:9-10. Write out these verses as a prayer for your husband. (For example, "Lord, I pray that my husband will not lie to me…")

_____

_____

_____

_____

_____

_____

_____

_____

10. Pray the prayer on page 184 in *The Power of a Praying Wife*. Include specifics about your husband's self-esteem.

WEEK TWENTY-NINE

Read chapter 29: "His Faith" from
The Power of a Praying Wife.

1. Do you see your husband as a man who walks in faith to a certain degree in his life? In what ways and to what degree?

    _____

    _____

    _____

    _____

2. Sensing our own limitations doesn't mean our faith is weak; feeling that *God* has limitations indicates weak faith. Do you think your husband believes that God has limitations? Explain. Write out a prayer asking God to help your husband believe that with God nothing is impossible.

    _____

    _____

    _____

    _____

    _____

    _____

    _____

3. Are you and your husband in agreement about faith in God? About belief in the Bible? Are you in unity about the church where you worship? Explain. How could you pray about these things?

_____

_____

_____

_____

_____

_____

_____

4. Is your husband's faith in God's love, protection, and ability to answer his prayers unwavering, or does he have times of serious doubt? Why? How do you feel about his level of faith? How would you like to see it change?

_____

_____

_____

_____

_____

_____

_____

_____

5. Read Matthew 17:20. Write out a prayer asking God to help
    your husband develop the kind of faith that moves mountains
    so that nothing will be impossible in his life. Pray that for your-
    self as well.

    _____

    _____

    _____

    _____

    _____

    _____

    _____

    _____

6. Do you believe that there is nothing in your life or your hus-
    band's life that can't be positively affected by having a stronger
    relationship with God and faith in His Word? Why or why not?
    What things in particular do you feel would be greatly affected
    by your husband having a stronger faith in God?

    _____

    _____

    _____

    _____

    _____

    _____

    _____

7. Read Ephesians 6:14-16. Why is the shield of faith important?

_____

_____

_____

_____

8. Read James 1:6-8. What kind of life are we setting ourselves up
   for if we are controlled by doubt?

_____

_____

_____

_____

9. Read Romans 10:17. If faith comes by hearing the Word of
   God, how could you pray for your husband to increase in faith?

_____

_____

_____

_____

10. Pray the prayer on page 189 in *The Power of a Praying Wife*.
    Include specifics about your husband's faith.

WEEK THIRTY

Read chapter 30: "His Hearing" from
The Power of a Praying Wife.

1. Read Matthew 13:13. Why did Jesus need to speak clearly to people in easy-to-understand stories?

    _____

    _____

    _____

    _____

2. Read John 8:43. Why didn't the people understand Jesus? In light of this Scripture, write out a prayer for both you and your husband to be able to hear God speaking to you from His Word.

    _____

    _____

    _____

    _____

    _____

    _____

    _____

    _____

3. Read Acts 13:16. What did Paul ask the people who fear God to do? Write out a prayer asking God to help you and your husband to do that as well. Ask God to help you build up your husband by assuring him that you trust his capability to hear from God, and you need him to trust your capability to do the same.

    _____

    _____

    _____

    _____

    _____

    _____

    _____

4. Read Proverbs 22:17. Write out this Scripture as a prayer for your husband. (For example, "Lord, I pray You would help my husband to incline his ear to hear…")

    _____

    _____

    _____

    _____

    _____

    _____

    _____

    _____

    _____

    _____

5. Read Isaiah 6:8-10. What did God tell the prophet Isaiah to tell the people? What would happen to the people if they didn't have dull hearts and closed ears and eyes? God did this because at a certain point of refusing to hear or see the truth, He gives people over to the consequences of their determination to rebel against Him. How could you pray for your husband in light of that?

_____

_____

_____

_____

6. Have you ever observed closed ears in your husband? Do you feel it has caused him to forfeit certain blessings because of that?

_____

_____

_____

_____

7. Read 1 John 4:6. Do you ever tell your husband something you feel is from God? Does he hear you when you do? In light of this Scripture, if you tell your husband something you feel is right and he does not hear you, what could this indicate? How could you pray about that?

_____

_____

_____

_____

8. Has there ever been a situation where your husband has not heeded your advice, or not considered your input, or did not do what you asked him to do, and there have been negative consequences because of it? Write out your answer as a prayer to God asking Him to redeem that situation and work forgiveness in your heart as well.

_____

_____

_____

_____

_____

9. Is there a situation right now where you need your husband to truly hear you regarding it, and you are either hesitant to talk to him about it, or you have already talked to him about it and he has not heard you concerning it? Write out your answer as a prayer asking God to open your husband's heart to hear from Him and to hear you as well regarding this issue.

_____

_____

_____

_____

_____

_____

10. Pray the prayer on page 194 in *The Power of a Praying Wife*. Include specifics about your husband's ability to hear from God and to truly hear you when you speak to him.

WEEK THIRTY-ONE

Read chapter 31: "His Future" from
The Power of a Praying Wife.

1. Does your husband feel hopeful about the future? Why or why not?

    _____

    _____

    _____

    _____

    _____

2. Does your husband have a vision for the future? In other words, even though he may not know specifics about his future, does he have a sense of the direction he's going in and feel good about it? Do you? Explain.

    _____

    _____

    _____

    _____

    _____

    _____

3. How do *you* feel about your husband's future? Are you concerned about it? Do you feel hopeful? Why or why not? What could you say to your husband today that would help him to feel hopeful about his future? How could you pray?

_____

_____

_____

_____

_____

_____

_____

_____

4. Does your husband have a tendency to get overworked, overtired, overwhelmed, burned out, distanced from God, or confused about his purpose? Explain why or why not.

_____

_____

_____

_____

_____

_____

_____

_____

5. Read Jeremiah 29:11. Does your husband ever lose sight of his dreams and forget what God says about his future? Explain. If so, how could you help him?

_____

_____

_____

_____

_____

_____

_____

_____

6. Read Romans 8:18. Do you or your husband ever forget the glory that is set before you when you are suffering in the present? Give examples. How could you pray about this?

_____

_____

_____

_____

_____

_____

_____

_____

7. Write down what you think concerns your husband most about his future. Now ask him and see what he says. Did he say the same things you thought he would say? Did he add anything that surprised you?

_____

_____

_____

_____

_____

_____

_____

_____

_____

8. Write out a prayer regarding everything your husband mentioned being concerned about for his future. Tell him you are going to be praying for each one of those concerns.

_____

_____

_____

_____

_____

_____

9. God doesn't want us to know the future. He wants us to know
   _____. (See page 199, last paragraph, in *The Power
   of a Praying Wife*.) If we do that, He can lead us into our future
   one step at a time. Write out a prayer for your husband to know
   Jesus better.

   _____

   _____

   _____

   _____

   _____

   _____

10. Pray the prayer on page 200 in *The Power of a Praying Wife*.
    Include specifics about your husband's future.

Answers to Prayer

What answers to prayer have you seen since you
started praying for your husband? Be sure to write
them down. It's important to acknowledge what
God has done and praise Him for it.

_____

_____

_____

_____

_____

_____

_____

_____

_____

_____

_____

_____

_____

_____

Answers to Prayer

Answers to Prayer

Other Books by Stormie Omartian

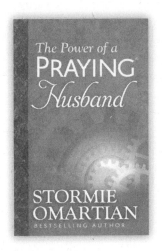

THE POWER OF A PRAYING® HUSBAND

Building on the success of *The Power of a Praying® Wife,* Stormie offers this guide to help husbands better understand their wives and pray for them more effectively. Each chapter provides biblical wisdom, insight, and powerful prayers, and the book features comments from well-known Christian men.

LEAD ME, HOLY SPIRIT

Stormie has written books on prayer that have helped millions of people talk to God. Now she focuses on the Holy Spirit and how He wants you to listen to His gentle leading when He speaks to your heart, soul, and spirit. He wants to help you enter into the relationship with God you yearn for and the wholeness and freedom He has for you. He wants to lead you into a better life than you could ever possibly live without Him.

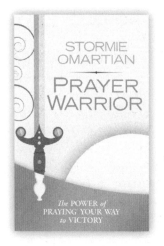

PRAYER WARRIOR

Stormie says, "There is already a war going on around you, and you are in it whether you want to be or not. There is a spiritual war of good and evil—between God and His enemy—and God wants us to stand strong on His side, the side that wins. We win the war when we pray in power because prayer *is* the battle." This book will help you become a powerful prayer warrior who understands the path to victory.

THE POWER OF PRAYER™ TO CHANGE YOUR MARRIAGE

When you invite the Lord to rule in your marriage, He will transform both of your lives in ways you never thought possible. This book addresses deeper issues such as communication breakdown, struggles with finances, the challenge of children, and various destructive attitudes and behaviors. If you want your marriage to be strong and protected, this book is for you. Learn how to pray so your marriage can last a lifetime.

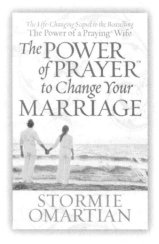

THE POWER OF PRAYING® FOR YOUR ADULT CHILDREN

Stormie Omartian says, "Our concern for our children does not stop once they step out in the world and leave home. If anything, it increases. There is much more to be concerned about, but as parents we have less influence over their lives than ever. Even so, there is a way to make a big difference in their lives every day, and that is through prayer." This book by Stormie will help every parent to pray powerfully for their adult children and find peace in the process.

JUST ENOUGH LIGHT FOR THE STEP I'M ON

Anyone going through changes or difficult times will appreciate Stormie's honesty, candor, and advice based on the Word of God and her experiences in this book, which is perfect for the pressures of today's world. She covers such topics as "Surviving Disappointment," "Walking in the Midst of the Overwhelming," "Reaching for God's Hand in Time of Loss," and "Maintaining a Passion for the Present" so you can "Move into the Future God Has for You."

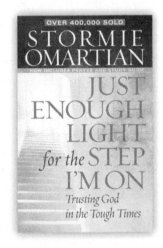